What the Country Wrought

What the Country Wrought

Annis Cassells

PURPLE DOOR PRESS

What the Country Wrought

Copyright 2023 by Annis Cassells

Interior design by Joan Raymond
Cover design by Cathy Walker
Cover art by Jonathan Swerdlick
Photo by Jill Hayner-Thompson

ISBN | Paperback: 979-8-9884111-0-9

All Rights Reserved.

No part of this publication may be reproduced, stored in a retrieval system, or transmitted, in any form by any means electronic, mechanical, or photocopying, recording or otherwise without the prior permission in writing from the author.

Contents

Part One
For All Who Have Been

Questions I Wish I'd Asked My Father	3
Five and Dime Memories	5
Time in the Saddle	7
Rivals in Dreamland	9
Setting Her Own Limits	11
Welcome Into the Fold	13
After Those Nineteen Children Were Killed in Texas	14
Postcard from the Marcy School Gym	16
First Friends	17
Auntie Harriet	19
A Question of Grace	21
Carolina Rest Stop	22
Snapshot of Nay	24
Homeland	25
The Whittler	27

Part Two
Any Curve That Comes My Way

Ode To Big Red	31
Thank You for Your Service	32
Bearing Witness	34
What the Country Wrought	36
The Joining	37
Coos Bay Apartment	38
The Hammock	40
Love Knows No Difference	42
Diving	44
We Put It All Together	48
Mayday in May 2020	50
Harvest	52
Summer of Truth, 1952	54
Ode to the American Black Cowboy	55

Simply This	57
Resilience	58

Part Three
Last Leg to Athens

I Never Knew I So Loved Annis	63
Sorority	67
Oh, My Hips	69
If only	71
In my dream	72
Asterisk	74
Behold September	76
The Hub	78
In the Community Garden	80
Twice Blessed	82
At the Amphitheater in Mission Dolores Park	84
Flawed Photos Must Suffice	85
2AM Contemplation	87
Morning Meditation	89
Now that I am older	90
Breather in Chapel Hill	92
I hold on	93
That Moment When We Call the Roll	94
Georgia Gauntlet – Atlanta to Athens	97
Notes	101
Acknowledgments	103
About the Author	105
Also by Annis Cassells	107

For all my Family:
born into, birthed, by marriage, and chosen

"Poetry is language against which you have no defenses."

— *David Whyte*

Part One

For All Who Have Been

Questions I Wish I'd Asked My Father

Where did you, the ninth child, sleep
in that small, brown-shingled home?

Who were your closest siblings, did they take
    care of you if you were hurt or sad
    did they play with you, make you laugh

Who got into the most trouble?

Do you remember your older sister
    who died of appendicitis
    before the doctor could arrive?

I want to know about your young life, those years
between 17 and 25 when you were on your own

    Who and what did you love?
    Did your yearning to become
    a musician come true?
    What hard lessons did you learn?

You worked as a driver. Who taught you,
and how did you feel teaching Tommy and me?

Remember that time you quit
    smoking for almost four years.
      Then took it up again?

                    Why?

How did you and Mama really meet?

    I know it wasn't on a slow boat to China
    like you always said.

Where did you get my name?

Five and Dime Memories

August, we take the streetcar downtown,
just Mama and me, to hunt for a pair of girlish
school shoes that fit my woman-sized feet,

low-heeled sturdies that could kick a soccer ball
or the 7th grade pest who tried to touch my breast,
and stay fastened on my boat-long tootsies.

Afterward, shoebox in hand, we make
our way to the big Woolworth's
on Detroit's Woodward Avenue

climb the wide, pink-marbled staircase
to the mezzanine lunch counter
slide onto side-by-side red swivel stools.

Mama reads the plastic-covered menu.
I flip the jukebox selections and hope
for a nickel. I don't ask.

The waitress in a cap-sleeved yellow dress
and apron stands before us, her pencil poised

above the order pad, almost sings *What'll it be?*

My order is always the same: A grilled cheese
sandwich and a chocolate malt, extra chocolate.
Mama orders coffee and some kind of sandwich.

She winks at me. Then I notice the nickel. It's
Buffalo side up. But I still call it good luck—
a jukebox nickel and Elvis singing "Hound Dog."

Time in the Saddle

Astride Big Red, my shiny, candy apple
Goldwing. Clutches out at first light.

We're about to cross Arizona's Sonoran
Desert, Ginny, Laurie, Sylvia, and me—
Our annual summer ride.

On other cross-country trips I cherish riding solo,
the powerful feeling that rises as I handle
both my bike and me in space and time,
make every decision. No compromises.

The journey's unfamiliar sights beckon me,
the freedom I long for, mine. I have time
to reckon with choices, time to remember triumphs
and setbacks, between a roadmap's dots and stars.

Big Red cruises in the staggered formation the four
of us favor. Her tires' metronomic slap serenades me
as rubber meets the dewy road then peels away.

The fringe on my chaps and jacket flutters, my
body a strobe atop the steadiness of the bike.

I look to the triangle of light that brightens,
expands between the lifting clouds and the crotch
of the hills ahead.

In hypnotic solitude, I wonder whose
imprints landed on this spot before mine,
where those folks started, where they ended up.

I look to the road's left-leaning curve before me.
I look inside my full heart—and know

I have everything I want and need. Know I
can ride any curve that comes my way

Rivals in Dreamland

I step out, arms swinging.
Soon leading the pack,
I take the wide concrete stairs
march on to victory.
"I Am Woman, Hear Me Roar"
crescendos in my head.

My face, impassive, strong, tilts upward.
My perfect nose points the path.
And the people follow. I hear them say

Thank God someone knows the way.

I reach for the brass handle
of the closed door and tug.
It doesn't open. I yank harder.

Behind us, Rita Mae Nash forges
through, like a storm trooper,
twists and pulls. Smirks.

It's all in the wrist.

She parades across
the threshold,
her silken neck swan-like,
her head diva high.

She, since 6th grade,
always in first.
Always more diva
than I.

Setting Her Own Limits

She never learned
the art of setting limits.

In her day
the woman had
no say
about what she
would,
could,
should,
or must not do.

In her younger days,
sheep-like she followed,
performed, steady
as a trained elephant,
met every expectation.

By the time she reached crone age
she'd stared down countless trials,
and tough decisions,
withstood widowhood.

She recognized her stature
began to honor her wisdom,
own her power, breathe rare air.

She spoke up.
Said no,
to everyone's surprise.
Said yes
to heartfelt desires,
cravings she hadn't known.

Carved out the rest of her days
With her own knife

Welcome Into the Fold

My heart, a tanka drum, bursts in my chest.
My mind, a kaleidoscope of scenarios, flashes
and flits, fickle as a larkspur, will not calm.

What are we doing here? I can't believe we didn't
apply the brakes before it became too late.
Before we made promises we dare not keep.

A horde of sisters flank us, not one smile among them.
And He, the stick-straight, bejeweled, self-proclaimed master preaching
service is our obligation, our destiny.

The ceremony begins. Spellbound, his goldens pack
the pews, their adoring faces welcome us into the fold.
For them, like them, we are enrolled, already pledged.

I push back, shed the stifling, good-girl shroud, grab
my friend's hand, and through the crowd, that sea
of stylish hats, we flee.

After Those Nineteen Children Were Killed in Texas

May 24, 2022

*To the Honorable Kevin McCarthy, Speaker,
House of Representatives of the United States*

Flags at half-mast – again.
Another school shooting in America.
Nineteen of our babies slaughtered in Uvalde.
The entire country traumatized—again.

Another school shooting in America,
another senseless loss for a generation.
Children across the country, traumatized—again.
How many more kids need to die, Kevin?

Another senseless loss for a generation
raised on active shooter drills and terror
They worry, we worry, Kevin, they will die
because of America's obsession with guns.

Raised on active shooter drills and fear,
their childhoods interrupted, stolen
because of America's obsession with guns,
and legislators' loyalties, their lack of guts.

Are you as heartbroken, repulsed, outraged as we
over those babies slaughtered? Do something, Mr.
House Leader. Make sure this is never again
why America's flags fly at half-mast.

Postcard from the Marcy School Gym

This gym looks a lot smaller now.
This place where I shrank from the path of the dodgeball.
This place where we do-si-doed every other Friday in 7th grade.
Here I am, looking out at the thick black lines that form
the rectangle that surrounds the basketball court,
the red circle that intrudes across the center line
that cuts the court in half, remembering the time I fell
full force into the yellow brick wall, knocking myself unconscious,
I awoke in in the ample arms of my teacher Mr. Sam Taub.
He was waving smelling salts beneath my nostrils. I peered
up beyond his freckled ski slope of a nose into his caring
brown eyes, in this place where Mr. Taub never let a child
be the last one chosen for a team or as a square dance partner.
My love of this place was never about the gym.

First Friends

For my brother Thomas

For a time we were each other's Universe. Took turns being the Sun the other revolved around. Basked in the thrown light, the brightness never too much to bear.

Childhood photos tell the story of before we can remember. The two of us in an open field. How our skinny bronzed legs arrowed into white socks that slumped over brown high top shoes, straw hats askew on our heads.

You oozed imagination: *How would it look if we took off this part? Or the wheels? What if we turned this around?* And you figured out how to skirt Mama's rules: *Mommy, you didn't say 'stay in the yard'* **this** *time!*

Riding Norman's two-wheeler after Daddy told you not to, you crashed and fell, scratched up your face and legs. Norman and I tried to cover your wounds with paper that matched your burnished brown skin, cut up one of his picture books, taped the cutouts to your body so no one would notice the wounds. The three of us marched downstairs, solemn as a peace delegation. Stopped mid-step when Daddy demanded, *What's wrong with your face!* We kids looked at each other in wonderment, as if to say *How did he know?*

In the apartment on Kenilworth, the nights we stretched our bodies off the edge of our beds, toes dug into our mattresses so we could truthfully say we were still in bed. We strained forward, our elbows braced on the cool linoleum floor. Then we could just barely hear Mama's radio stories from the front room.

The day you, a kindergartner, tried to smuggle two cents out for an after-school candy store stop. You put one penny in each coat pocket so they wouldn't clink against each other when Mama buttoned your coat. For some reason (mother's intuition?) she checked your pockets, and you were discovered. I remember thinking *that was so smart of him.*

Those carefree growing up years in Columbus we ranged the neighborhood, barefoot on rainy days, in rubber boots through snow and slush. Our only tethers, growling stomachs and illuminated streetlights. Summertime meant a bushel basket of home grown tomatoes on the back porch, Double Dutch and Hide 'n Seek with friends on our block, bicycling to the end of Mooberry Street.

We outgrew childhood, began to orbit distant Suns, forged our own paths. Our lives—jobs, family, location, interests—different, but bright constellations, still shimmering with our parents' values.

Now we are the elders. Standing back, we observe the young ones. We know when to speak up and when to be silent — wisdom hard won, gleaned over decades sprinkled with stardust and grit.

Auntie Harriet

This here yo' great, great aunt Harriet.

These words. This woman
Harriet my ancestor.
I'm her legacy.

Of regal presence
Her eyes, aflame, engender
Trust, call me to follow.

May I take courage
From this invincible woman
May I do her proud

How will I stand strong,
Match her bravery, march forth
On a fierce moral path

Strike out oppression
Seek universal justice
Insist on its reign

For all who have been
Denied, denigrated, shoved
To ev'ry line's end.

A Question of Grace

I sit at the heart
of our spiritual community,
Inspire's Sunday Service.
Today's sermon is on mercy.
I take in the teaching, open
to the idea of grace
grasp that I have received grace
in seasons of despair and worry
after mistakes and misjudgments
in times of happiness and success—
all my life.

I understand I must learn
to extend Grace—
Even if it's inconvenient.
Even if my sensibilities are shaken.
Even if I'm still mad as hell.
If the heartbreak stings even now.
Even if that grace is to myself.

Carolina Rest Stop

I stand slightly bent over
in the roadside parking lot.
My teeth sink through

fuzzy, vermilion-colored skin
to firm golden flesh. Sticky juice
makes tracks forearms to elbows.

By what chance might two travelers
have struck up a restroom conversation
and I would taste my first Georgia peach?

We meet at the wash basins
Eye each other in the wall-wide mirror.
Our voices bounce from our reflections.

Her drawl drifts
from her wrinkled lip-sticked mouth.
My twang peals
from between pecan-colored lips.

We pass pleasantries between us, amble
out together side-by-side. Her voice brings
memories of childhood next-door neighbors
who migrated north to Detroit.

I say
They spoke of someone
Or some thing
Sweet as a Georgia peach

Her beckoning fingers say
"come with me."
And I follow.

Snapshot of Nay

In memory of my sister Reenié, 1950-2019

If you'd had my sister — lip-locked keeper
of secrets, persistent funny-bone tickler,
lender of clothes and jewels, the baby—
buffer between parents and sibs—
rapid-fire wielder of snappy come backs,
ace distractor from boring chores,
inventor of the deluxe Sister Sandwich,
devoted guardian of her loved ones'
best interests, queen of the fairways &
General Motors Knowledge Center,
unique vessel holding
the family memory, ardent lover
of *Blazing Saddles* and those who rolled
in the aisles along with her—you would
have been favored with a divine essence
for sustaining joy.

Homeland

The Nairobi airport
churns, throbs, pulses
with folks who look like me.
Bag handlers, flight crews

somebodies in charge, shopkeepers.
Black people making everything
happen. Black bodies work
together, make everything go.

Dropped among, surrounded by
unknown brothers and sisters
I recognize a hunger
blooming in my gut.

My voice chokes with tears
as I hand over my passport
to the customs officer in his booth.

He raises his head, smiles. *Jambo!*
Looks like you've been here before.
Welcome home!

Throughout the Kenyan highlands
in the depths of the Ngorngoro Crater
across the plains of the Serengeti,

smiles widen on Kenyan faces
heads nod, eyes register kinship,
recognition of this Sister

the single safari traveler
who shares their roots

Looks like you been here before.
Welcome home!

The Whittler

Winter nights GrandPap sat
snug near the coal stove

in the home-place dining room
a cone of hops tucked in his cheek.

Arthritic fingers wrapped around
a time-worn pocketknife,

he scored a dark scantling of tinder
with knife point markings true.

His opening cleave
unlocked the wood's walnut breath.

Silent shavings lined his lap,
surrounded his straight-backed chair

'til bedtime, when GrandPap pushed
forward the perfect chain he'd carved.

Part Two

Any Curve That Comes My Way

Ode To Big Red

This week I tossed away the yard-long coiled lock, heavy black vinyl over thick corded wire, the one I bought for us for that trip into Mexico so we could tether your front wheel to the wheel of the bike parked beside us, each motorcycle secured to the one next to it, our attempt to thwart thieves and keep everyone on the road for that breathtaking ride, billed as an "all-women's tour with a few good men," an adventure in which you taught me to stay upright moving through gravel to get to the Pemex fuel pumps and stop with assurance to keep the rubber side down, as motorcyclists say when they mean "no crashing"; to creep through the *vados*, especially after a rain as we never knew what obstacle might be lying in wait on the bottom to ensnare us and bring us down.

We took the curves smooth as a do-si-do, and with my map taped to your dash, traversed the Baja Peninsula, all the way down and back to that middle-of-nowhere checkpoint where boys looking no older than my middle school students, those boys who talked so brave but were afraid to step on the foot-peg to sit in your saddle since only your thin steel kickstand held you up, but these sullen Mexican boy-soldiers, real rifles hoisted on their shoulders, ordering us to halt so they could search us and our bikes for drugs before allowing us to proceed up the dusty road toward the USA, didn't faze us. You always brought us home, Big Red.

Thank You for Your Service

Who could know that after Pearl Harbor
my Ohio farm-raised uncles would enlist,

proud to be Army and Navy bound,
to defend their country, and who could know

they'd march into World War II,
relegated to segregated units,

except, on European soil they'd
stand taller, tread lighter

not shunned or shamed
not damned or diminished,

but respected as Americans
accepted as men

would shelter and fight in foxholes
with white soldiers, break bread --

and return home heroes, hoisted
high on their countrymen's shoulders

as if the U.S. had changed, as if
the home-front war was done raging.

After the homecoming parade, after the
champagne and welcome home speeches,

it was business as usual.

Bearing Witness

The red light whirled and flashed on this residential tree-lined street near Detroit. Not my normal route, but a diversion, a road less taken. The vested officer, shimmered in the noon-time heat, loomed tall beside the window of a maroon Mini-Cooper. The driver's license in hand, he retreated to his silver-and-white Beverly Hills Police Department SUV.

I strolled past the cop and the car. Glanced over to see a young Black man, the driver, a young Asian woman in the passenger's seat. Both mute. He with jaw clenched, hands clutching the wheel. She held herself tight, arms around her waist, rocked back and forth. I acknowledged them with a nod and *hey there* as I passed.

Fifty yards further, in an oasis of shade I took out my phone, brought up the camera, to wait while the scene played out. A second police car approached. The two armed officers strutted in synch, surrounded the Mini-Cooper. Rooted to the steaming asphalt, I stood beneath that tree, focused, held my packages and my breath. Exhaled once the officer pulled away.

. . .

The Mini-Cooper remained still for twenty heartbeats. It inched away from the curb, commenced forward, stopped beside me. The young driver met my gaze, reached out his hand, shook mine. *Thank you. Thank you for waiting.*

What the Country Wrought

From our home in Detroit, we kids called it "down in the country"— that tiny Ohio farm where our dad was born and raised. An even dozen siblings at the table. Crops of tomatoes, potatoes, kohlrabi, corn, and hops in the garden. His round-cheeked mother at the iron cookstove. Where we fetched clear, cool spring water uphill for drinking, cooking, bathing. My grandparents' adage: *many hands make light work*. The final child of that hardy generation, 101 years old, died this year. The homeplace empty, derelict, returned to earth— like all of them.

down home country
memory-filled
family legacy

The Joining

I emerge from the Eugene Airport
jetway and spot her.
The deep red of her jacket reflects
in her flushed face.
Arms flung wide, she enfolds me.
A boulder in the river
of passengers
wheeling their carry-ons,
lugging their duffels,
we force the flow around us.
After months of long-distance
conversations, letters, chats.
Together now,
two women seeking happiness.
There is only us.

Coos Bay Apartment

We return for the summer.
Our best friends' handmade welcome banner
Is affixed to the fern-green door.
Judy slides the key into the lock.

The place has paused, just as we left it last
Fall. Chairs huddle beneath plastic drop cloths.
Assorted rain jackets are crammed in closets,
A-1 Sauce and French's mustard in the fridge.

We need to clean
Restock the pantry
Hook up the wi-fi and cable.
But we are home

To our knickknacks and books
Funky artwork on the walls
The Craig's List leather love seat
New towels we bought last year.

Home croons to me of childhood,
Of times forgotten and remembered

Game nights over dominoes and cards
Schoolwork, apple pies, and lentil soup
On the lemon-yellow Formica table

Home, a sense of belonging,
A warmth I feel in my core
A comfort, like being wrapped
In my mother's soft chenille robe,
Scooped up and hugged.

The Hammock

Cradled in canvas
on their hillside in rural Ohio
our GrandPap often slept
in mid-day sprawl beneath
two sturdy trees.
The hammock's subtle shifts
matched his measured breath.

Sometimes the hammock strained—
when we grandkids piled in,
over-filled the wide sling, pumped
and swung to nearly upside down
like airplane stunt fliers.
Bark-rubbed ropes sang their song,
squeaked in rhythm with us city
kids' pumps and whoops.

My last time in the hammock,
Grandma had died. With GrandPap
comforted by other family, we cousins
mustered on the scuffed hillside,

the grass worn to dirt. Tears and humid
air dampened our faces as we told
favorite "Mom" stories, paired up
for turns, gently swung
the hammock with our toes.

Love Knows No Difference

When my friend found her true self, I hadn't met her yet. Didn't know she had searched for the connection to her past, to the time before she came into the family I knew.

She knew she was adopted, but photos and mirrors placed differences before her eyes, set her to wondering the why and where-from of her golden skin and night-black hair.

So, she asked.

Her mother said *Wait here,* walked away, stayed away for what seemed like a very long time. When she returned, her mother cradled a bright red blanket not so big, but big enough to wrap an infant among the wide, bright chevrons, red, black, and gold, woven into the fabric.

You came to us gift-wrapped in this blanket. Snug and warm, safe. She handed the folded blanket to her daughter. *This told us you were loved, told us whoever released you loved you enough to let you go.*

Right then, you were our daughter. Ours, every bit as much as whoever enfolded you and entrusted you to us.

Diving

I watch from my window as a man wearing jeans and red suspenders lifts himself and hangs on the side of the dumpster, climbs in. He emerges with a four-legged piece of metal. Heavy wire, like a yard sign support. He extracts a tool from his pocket, maybe pliers, attempts to dismantle the piece. But it's no use. So he presses the legs together, forms a long instrument, forked on both ends. He holds it like a sword, as if in defense mode, or attack. His somber face screws into menacing. He spars with an invisible foe.

I assume dumpster divers are homeless people.
Homeless. Unhomed. Houseless. Unhoused.
Experiencing housing insecurity.

- More than half a million people in the U.S. are houseless.
- Young adults aged 24-50 make up 70% of homeless persons.

Sir? I say as I drive up and address a man rifling through the plastic garbage bags in the dumpster then pitching found items into his metal mesh wagon. He looks up from beneath the bill of his black ballcap. I say, *Would you please be sure to close the lid when you're finished.* With an I-already-know-that manner and his forearm, which bears a tattoo of an inked-in cross, he waves me off.

    1. **haul** (verb) to take from one place to another
       Synonyms: bear, carry, ferry, lug, pack, tote

I was sitting in a taxi, wondering if I had overdressed for the evening, when I looked out the window and saw Mom rooting through a Dumpster. ~ Jeannette Walls in *The Glass Castle, A Memoir*

- 30% of homeless people in America are women.

Six-thirty a.m. and someone's inside the dumpster. I notice a pink collar above the camo-print jacket. The person seems smaller in stature. And then I see curls wisping out from a black skullcap. I wonder if this is the girl I've encountered before. Petite hands pitch out a small hoop.

It is the girl. She sits up on the edge of the dumpster, swings her legs around then jumps down. She wipes her hands on a black cloth that hangs off the front and tosses it back in. She closes the lid. I recall the time before—she told me she always left things neat. The girl wiggles into her backpack then heaves her large, black plastic bag onto her shoulder.

1. ***haul*** (noun) the total amount collected
or obtained especially at one time
Synonyms: bounty, cargo, catch, load, take, yield

The term for those who collect and sell used bottles and cans they have found in recycling bins and dumpsters is ***binners.***

One time, a binner explained to me, *At least I'm helping the environment by recycling!*

- Over 20% of homeless people are kids.

Dear Girl in the Dumpster,
We spoke one day when I came upon you at the dumpster. I think about your haunted eyes. I wonder about you—what circumstances made this life your only option. I wonder whether it **is** your only option. No kid says *I'm gonna be a dumpster diver when I grow up.* I wonder what you dreamed of being.

Q & A
Is dumpster diving legal?
Illegal at WalMarts across the country. And Texas. *Texas?*
Legal in California since the state Supreme Court ruled in 1988. But divers can be arrested or fined if they trespass or litter.
Legal in Nevada and Oregon.
Legal in Chicago. But divers are required to get a license and pay $50 per year for their permit in other Illinois cities.

One morning, a man pedals his bike toward
Me. I'm carrying our empty green recycle bin.
He approaches and says:
Uh, is it okay if I go through the dumpster?
I wonder: Do I look like I'm in charge here?
Me: *Not really, sir. But please,*
close the lid when you're done.

We Put It All Together

The battered box, held together with blue painter's tape,
contained a jigsaw puzzle left over from the summer before.

The photograph showed a collage of glass, colored and shaped
by constant tumbling in ocean waves. It promised a challenge.

Perfect from all directions. The orientation didn't matter.
We decided which side was up and got to work, sorting.

Found and joined the straight-edged pieces, the border.
An upper corner was missing. No matter, we carried on.

Discovered the pieces near the absent corner, stabilized it.
Matched the hazy, the bright, and the rippled broken

glass pieces that melded together. Bent to complete
the picture. Sometimes we could discern a soda bottle

neck or mouth, sometimes a brown shard from a beer bottle
or a green one from wine. Parts resembling lapis popped up

in unexpected places. We didn't try to guess their origins, simply
noticed them and focused on putting the puzzle together.

We dismissed two distinctly odd pieces that didn't fit, wondered
if they even belonged, where they came from. We grumbled

when pieces we tried didn't work. Lamented when searches
for obvious ones rendered nothing. Cheered each success.

At the end, three pieces were nowhere to be found. Their spaces glared
empty, unfulfilled. We stepped back, surveyed our work. Noticed,

like our lives, the original pieces had transformed into something
beautiful and gratifying together. Some might say, remarkable.

Mayday in May 2020

Overnight
I became elderly

Vulnerable
Susceptible to the virus

Killing young and old—
Mostly old

At the supermarket
Disinfectant

Masks and gloves
Out of stock

Limits on hand
Sanitizer and bleach

Shelves marked toilet paper
A bare-faced lie

I scrawled my name in the dust
On those forlorn surfaces

Overnight
I became expendable

Because the economy
Because the right to haircuts

And beach bonfires
Because beers at the pub
Because some freedoms matter more

Because
Seniors should just stay *inside*
We're gonna die anyway

I don't feel elderly
I don't feel expendable

What I do feel
Is fervent desire

To knock common sense
Into virus deniers, menacing

Unmasked protesters brandishing
Rifles and pistols, sardined
On the Capitol steps.

Harvest

Vegetable-laden table before me
Two canners on the old gas stove
Ready to be filled with the next batch

Tears roll down my cheeks
Into a heaped porcelain bowl
This task I do not relish

This year my husband decides
To return to his roots, leases
Out-of-town land to farm

Never before, in the early years of raising
Kids, straining to make ends meet
There's no tillable land near asphalt streets

Now he plants and plants and plants, grows
Everything he remembers from childhood
Lugs all of it home, earth caked

Drops it in front of me, proud as a mouser
I'm surprised he's not pounding his chest

With both fists. He and his crops have defeated

Drought, infestation, too much sun,
Too little sun, too little faith. And now
It's left to me to fill cupboard shelves

With Mason jars—quarts crammed with food
He grew and harvested—to preserve
September tomatoes for March spaghetti.

Summer of Truth, 1952

We three lying 9-year-olds, Kay, David and me,
each pleading for a dime for ice cream, but plotting
to buy a pack of Camels and a packet of Sen-Sens,
imagining ourselves cool and hip like our parents.
Instead, puffing and coughing, hiding our stash
in an old purse, believing we can fool our mothers,
then discovering we are dead wrong.
And me, languishing, waiting
for the lecture that never comes—my mother,
wearing a tiny smile, silently tilting back and forth
in the wicker rocking chair on our red-floored porch.

Ode to the American Black Cowboy

You rode and wrangled and ran the cattle
of former enslavers, who, after Emancipation,
were bound by law to hire and pay you.

Your numbers would grow to one quarter
of the cowhands riding the range, driving cattle north.
And true to southern customs, they'd call you cow*boys*.

Equality emerged when, weapons drawn, all cowhands
clashed with rustlers, stood together and fought—
their only concern, the herd, not who was Black or White.

You are the likes of John Ware, Nat Love, Bill Pickett,
men born into slavery who headed west for opportunity.
You rode and roped and branded, performed in rodeos

and wild west shows across the nation and abroad.
And who could conceive of Bass Reeves, the first
Black deputy U.S. Marshal, among your number.

At Saturday matinees, we kids saw plenty of heroes
on horses, rodeo cowboys, sharpshooters, and

guitar-strumming dandies in fancy chaps and fringe.

But we never saw you.

None of us could imagine or admire you—couldn't look up
to you—as the heroes of our youth.

History overlooked you, excluded you in the lexicon
of the Old West, withheld your worth. We were denied
your example, stripped of our right to ancestral pride.

Today we witness your real place in our history—
realize and respect your triumphs, your achievements.
American Black cowboy, *our children* will know you.

Simply This

We ought to be able
To go to the store
Wait for the school bus and more,
An outdoor café, a table
For two or possibly four
And careless as a newborn
Not worry about a shot
Or a dozen, or sixty-five
Or if we'll even be alive
To greet a fresh morning

Your unchecked anger, hate and dread,
Fear turned within, flame strong—
Sear, consume your spark, the song
Of yourself you hold in your head.

You are the changer
and the changed.
No one is left unscathed.

Resilience

The crush comes swiftly—
suffocating,
devastating.
In that moment
of fragility,
of vulnerability,
the frenzied heart thumps,
pumping blood
to your uncomprehending brain.

The crush lifts slowly.
It just takes time.
Watch for the return of life,
not as you once knew it
but new
and good.

        You begin to rise.
        And if you can't
        yet stand tall
        step forward
        or feint sideways,

dig into the earth
with one elbow
then the other.
Drag yourself an inch or two ahead
like the downed soldier you are.
Whatever it takes
know you are enough.

Watch for the return of life,
not as you once knew it
but new and good
and worth the effort
Baby steps
or inch-by-inch
it's all forward.

                                          And in that moment
                                   when passion returns,
                                   overruns the heart's
                                  hysteria, overtakes
                            the clouded-over brain,
                                      you see the light,
                                the path to acceptance,
                                             to peace
                                     within yourself.

                                            You know you
                                            are enough
                                           to overcome
                                     whatever comes.

Part Three

Last Leg to Athens

I Never Knew I So Loved Annis

After Dean Rader

Someday I'll love Annis

                               the way a gnat

loves fruit ripening on the counter
or perhaps the way the moon loves the earth, teasing
doling itself out bit by bit

                               each month to turn

around and do it all again.

                   Someday I'll love my teeth, themselves

a marvel,

for they have experienced myriad cracks
and cavities

their depths and shapes as varied

                                                                       as potholes

in the streets of the Motor City
and likewise filled with cement

I dream will last.

                                                                  I never knew I

loved my fleshy knees.
Why did I inherit *those* parts of my mother?

I never knew I loved
my outrage.

Once on a flight to Detroit a pregnant woman beside me was ill
and I still remember
how heat flared in my neck

                       when the flight crew had no
                       blanket for her.

Then I dug into my bag for the cover I always carry.

                                I
                            never knew

I so loved my arms until they held both my children
cuddled on the balcony at my mother's house,

                        their limbs tucked like
                        new fawns'

beneath them. I like comparing my girls to fawns,
as they have known what it is to be protected,

                        to be new
                        to be loved.

Someday I will love the silence,

                                      the way I will love being

myself,

but this is not what I want to say.
It is something more like this:

                                        The future is not what we

                        dreamed it would be,

and that is only part of it.
The other part has something to do with what

                        we make it,

like what we create while we are in this realm.

I remember my mother's mother
would put her pressure cooker on the stove,

      Say *Come on, Baby*

grab my 4-year-old hand

          and take me to sit in the garden

until the danger of explosion was past.
I remember naming the hollyhocks and gladiolas.

      I loved
      those times.

Sorority

Sisters, let us mount up,
ride those long gone escapades
again. Indeed, we can resurrect
our heyday. We'll push
the memory gauge back
through those Iron Butt years,
when we rode two
columns wide, stretched out
on the highway, waved
at slack-jawed gawkers.
When Trudy pulled her bike up
short, blocked the intersection
so our cavalcade could safely pass.
When little girls
and women, too,
said they wanted
to be us
when they grew up.
Let's drag out cracked
photos, tatters of maps
holey Ride-In tee-shirts from

Boise, Eureka Springs, Boyne,
And in the remembering
celebrate our badass selves.

Oh, My Hips

After Lucille Clifton

These hips never fail me
though they sometimes disappoint
in their too-wideness—
a family trait handed down
generation upon generation

But these impassioned hips
squatted behind batter's boxes
stewed in study and meditation
sheltered two daughters
slingshot into skirmishes
survived in a world pierced by injustice
straddled fences, lines, and lovers

These hallowed hips linger
in memories of admirers,
disciples of juicy bottoms,
long after they look away,
murmur *have mercy*

These hips
once taut as a trampoline
now sprawl... settle... spread
become pillows
prop my beloved's head
while she reads

If only

For Reenié

dear Sister, I could get back
this moment: my hands
in your curls like the girls
we once were, playing house
and I am the mom saying *shush
now, you got nothin' to cry about*
and you, grumbling a moment more
then quiet, a kitten caressed,
purring with each stroke
of Mama's boar bristle brush.

In my dream

the horses—
swift and huge
their hooves
pound the earth
raise clods
fill the air
with dust.
But I
a city girl
am not afraid.
I'm drawn
to these glistening
muscled beings
their thick necks
graceful
their high heads
eclipsing the sun.

Then I wake up
in The Motor City—
reinforced concrete
and shiny steel

darken the sky.
On the streetscape
plastic, steel, and chrome
cars and trucks scurry,
like cockroaches
when the lights come on.

I turn over
conjure the horses—
mount
one halcyon steed
and ride away

Asterisk

To the clerk who schooled me on the real world

If I believe anything, it's that I must have conveyed confidence, maturity, a presence. I strode through the swinging, glass-windowed door of the Cass Technical High School office clutching my Senior Trip deposit. Twenty-five dollars.

I stated my name. You opened a black three-ring binder. Down the page you ran your index finger, poised it below my last name. I inquired about the asterisk. The one in the margin, before the C of Cassells. Asked why it was there. And you told me.

My skin prickled, and I wondered aloud why it mattered who the colored kids were. Required you to look me in the eye. Held your gaze, an invisible thread between us. Perspiration broke out below the bridge of your cat-eye glasses, beneath your nose, darkened your faint bleached-blond mustache.

Your lips spoke a truth of 1960: *We have to know who the colored kids are so we can assign roommates properly.*

My body went rigid. My heart quickened. I had nothing more to ask or say. Neither did you.

Behold September

after Lucia Perillo

The children have returned to in-person school—
after many months of virtual learning. Expectant

faces, new backpacks, new shoes mark the day
our youth reclaim their place in halls and classrooms.

And if the school is a cathedral and First Day is Sunday,
the kids are stained glass windows reflecting light.

Or say the school is an arena with ropes and silks
and lyra hanging from the rafters. Then the children

are daring aerialists harnessing their momentum.
Or if the school is a theater, the kids are the playwrights,

directors, stagehands, dancers, and actors.
Or let's say the school is a fertile garden.

Then the students are baskets, open vessels
destined to harvest skills, knowledge, and joy,

to be guided row by row, to gather those
essentials that will nourish and sustain a life.

The Hub

August 2022, and the Coos Bay Library
is now back at pre-pandemic operation.

Hushed voices stream from gleaming
wood tables, newly reinstated. I inhale

the aroma of books. This Library,
with its industrial-tiled floor, traffic-worn

carpet, and island of computer stations
necessary as oxygen, welcomes all.

An old man shows up for his daily dose
of respect. He hobbles in, long-haired, faded

blue jeans rumpling from beneath
a tattered tweed jacket. He jabs

his cane before each faltering step,
loud plunks echo on the tile.

He growls he needs his phone
charged. He needs to call Social Security.

Ref-Desk Paul appears, his voice calming
as a groomsman's to a skittish horse, eyes

fixed on the man's crumpled face. He notices
the phone and guides the man to a table

equipped with built-in electrical outlets.
While the man fumbles into a seat

Paul steadies the chair. He takes the
tangled phone cords, plugs in the phone

places a feather-light hand on the man's
shoulder: *There. You okay now, Marvin?*

In the Community Garden

She descends three steps
into the garden

A wide wooden bench
invites her to sit

Soak in sunshine
like the parsnips

Like the pink hydrangeas
the nearby chard and kale

Twists of gray dreadlocks
escape beneath the brim

of her wilted straw hat, her clouded
eyes rise above the red plaid mask

Wander past bloom-filled rows
in raised beds. Her gaze lingers

on bent backs, a family with two
Kids watering and weeding

She sees herself once more
in her own earlier gardens

Baskets heaped with bounty
she planted, tended and picked

Today in this community garden
her withered fingers pluck

Air flowers, pick imagined lint—
until one of the children

Places a yellow bouquet
in her chestnut hands

Twice Blessed

for Asila and Amina

When your daughter reads your poem aloud on New Year's
Day, and it's the first time you've heard it read by someone else
A tenderness blossoms, blooms, permeates your chest

When your daughter generously offers her Reiki Bliss Blast
Radiates love to friends and strangers, to the world at large
You swell with pride as hands around the globe raise, wave

When your daughter is one whom others seek for help
Her innate wisdom recognized, her counsel valued
When she sows seeds of compassion, inclusion, and grace

When your daughter leads the service at Inspire, welcomes
the congregation in her sincere glad-to-see-you voice
Begins the meditation, *Exhale everything before this moment*

When your daughters have the courage to live in authenticity
Strike out on their own, work to realize their dreams

Commit to building lives of purpose and personal meaning

When your daughters consider you, your passions, your needs
Support you when you set out in pursuit of your heartfelt desire
Pose perfect questions as you determine if, and how, to proceed

When your daughters and you survive a record worst year:
Their aunt dies of cancer, the pandemic strikes, Black lives
Still matter less in the USA, homes and lives are lost to wildfires

When life seems unmanageable, you have your daughters
The beautiful children you birthed, still nurture, celebrate, admire
Reminders the world is wondrous—love's strength, profound.

At the Amphitheater in Mission Dolores Park

In the bowl of the park, the actors
gather, costumed, ready to perform.
Spectators spread blankets,
top them with tablecloths, set out picnics.
Sunlight filters through clouds, kisses
green grass stage. And we are here,
you and I, camped on our own
tiny island of plaid, the stage
where we play out the prelude
to the next 50 years.

Flawed Photos Must Suffice

Fireworks soar heavenward. And the noise. On ascension, high-pitched like warheads. The eruptions rattle the night. Starbursts and Fountains, Chrysanthemums and Crossettes bloom across the sky, dissolve into gold and silver streams, cascade onto the bay.

We perch high above the bay on Telegraph Drive, 4th of July, the annual gathering of friends. We convene at eight, enjoy food and wine, chat 'til nearly ten. We nestle in at our hosts' column of picture windows when the northern sky tends dark enough to showcase China's gift to the world—their discovery that bamboo tossed into fire explodes. The Chinese launched these missiles to ward off evil spirits. Since 1777, America has set off fireworks to celebrate "our" independence.

But fireworks do not save us from the demon of disease. Liberty means nothing in the Pandemic of 2020—when the entire world becomes a chain of infection, when we stale in lockdown, when freedom becomes a luxury.

Today's memories are bungled photos saved on my cell phone. I scroll through thousands, seek remnants of past fourths of July when I was always a bit too late to snap the perfect shot—the design at its zenith.

2AM Contemplation

Perhaps an app,
a checklist to remind me

of these pre-deathbed chores:

Create a spreadsheet of passwords and codes.
Throw away keys to locks long-gone.
Update my obituary.
Make the rounds,
see the friends who are left.
Bury all hatchets.
Burn the journals.

Burn the journals.
Bury all hatchets.
See the friends who are left,
make the rounds.
Update my obituary.
Throw away keys to locks long-gone.
Create a spreadsheet of passwords and codes.

And about these pre-deathbed chores —
to remind me, a checklist.

Perhaps an app.

Morning Meditation

Mind and body comprehend the drill
Make a nest, get comfy, become still
discern the turmoil inside and out,
notice all the sounds. Without a doubt
snow geese overhead, their shrill honks blend
with traffic and a mower's hum as I transcend
into calm. Solitude refills the reservoir of one
whose life waves with battles lost and won
a nurturer whose calling in this life
is woman, mother, teacher, friend and wife
Thoughts come and go, spill into the silence
I invoke my divine and wait for guidance.

Now that I am older

I see virtue in vulnerability, feel perfection's
grasp slip, now can say

I don't know
and *I was wrong*

I hear my body speak the truth of past
abuse when muscles mock, reject commands

I taste a new-found sweetness recalling
times once bitter—or bland

I smell possibility in morning's dawning
find crusts of kindness as fists unfurl

I caress deep memories of loved ones
and keepsakes from long-gone days

I see other people's realities
garner new understandings

I hear tolerance in my heart as waxed,
rib-perched words hover, remain inside

I taste the fragility of life, create and
savor precious time with those I love

Breather in Chapel Hill

Crisp November air attempts to pierce my puffy Costco coat. I am trekking to the UNC campus, where I will address a class this morning. The students have read my book. Their pre-class questions and observations fight for space in my head alongside the snapshot of my sister. Alongside the logistics of changing home-going plans, the diversion to Detroit, where she lies dying. I step into the austere classroom. Grief slides over. Gives way to decades of carrying on. I home in on the faces, young, expectant. The smooth hands cradling my book. Fifty minutes. Respite from fear and my heavy heartful of loss. In closing, I read my poem "Resilience."

I hold on

to the bubbling beauty
and sorrows
of my life.
They reside
in sun-bleached memory
return
no matter how deep
the river of my wish
drift beyond
strung-together miles.
I hold and carry them all
scrawl haunting whirlwind days
in countless journals
morsels to be someday
savored denied
or burned.

That Moment When We Call the Roll

Each time a girl opens a book and reads a womanless history, she learns she is worth less.
~Myra Pollack Sadker

Disenfranchised
and discounted,
women organized,
fought, forged ahead,
showed up.

Lucretia and Elizabeth crusaded
for abolition and women's rights
Susan campaigned for suffrage
Alice led protests
Ida B. wrote [and marched, anyway]

Phoebe penned a letter
to a Tennessee state senator:
"Dear Son... Hurry and vote
for suffrage ... be a good boy."

And, red rose in his lapel,
he obeyed his mother,
cast the tiebreaker,
secured the right
to vote
for some women.

And after that
Shirley brought her own seat
to the table

Bella introduced the first
gay rights bill in Congress

Barbara orated with eloquence
in Texas & the House

Hillary advised
a President or two

Ruth fought
for gender equality

Nancy struck her Speaker's gavel
Elizabeth persisted—*nevertheless.*

Stacey rallied Georgia voters
Maxine reclaimed her time

Mazie served in both Houses
Kamala ran in Chuck Taylors—
and won.

Now,
Karen leads Los Angeles
Gretchen governs Michigan
Katanji sits with the Supremes

A womanless history no more,
I am making a record of their names.

May every girl know *her* place.

Georgia Gauntlet – Atlanta to Athens

High noon
Four friends bound for Athens
Astride iron and plastic steeds

        Candy apple red, yellow,
        metallic blue and black

We navigate Atlanta freeways
Our gloved fingers pythons
Squeeze the handlebars to death

Shirley leads
She honed her riding chops
in Los Angeles traffic

        She says to move as a block,
        A unit, an imaginary box
        At a safe distance, but close
        Allow no penetration

We sashay
Between lanes

Fearless as matadors
Over the unforgiving pavement
I-20 East to 85 North
Then highway 285 toward Athens
Where traffic clears

We exit
To a fast food chicken shack
Slow to a halt and park
Rip off our helmets and scream

We all scream
Shake out our hair and laugh
Stamp our feet like cartoon bulls
Shout all at once
we survived

We amble
Toward the door
Enter to rousing applause
Whoops and laughter
One teen worker jumps in place
Hollers
We ain't never seen no
Four women ride up
on no motorcycles before!

We swagger
Up to the counter
Like Tombstone gunslingers
Order fried chicken and biscuits
Enough to tide us over
For the last leg to Athens

Poetry calls us to pause. There is so much we overlook, while the abundance around us continues to shimmer, on its own.
—Naomi Shihab Nye—

Notes

Ekphrastic poems, inspired by works of art:

"Questions I Wished I'd Asked My Father" (Benode Behari Mukherjee. *Reclining Man*, 1957.)
"Five and Dime Memories" (Robert Frank. "Drug Store—Detroit", 1955.)
"Time in the Saddle" (Albert Watson. "Isle of Skye Road, Scotland", 2013.)
"Setting Her Own Limits" (Elaine Dunham. Exhibit flyer, "Setting Her Own Limits", 2019.)
"Welcome Into the Fold" (Aisha Galimbaeva. *At the Yurt*, 1990.)
"Auntie Harriet" (Bisa Butler. Textiles-Quilt, *I Go to Prepare a Place for You*, 2021.)
"Ode To Big Red" (Bernice Bing. *A Lady and a Roadmap*, 1962.)
"Love Knows No Difference" (Ruth Asawa. *Untitled*, 1948.)
"Harvest" (Vanessa Bell. *The Kitchen at Charleston, East Sussex*, 1943.)
"If only" (Carrie Mae Weems. "Woman Brushing Hair", Kitchen Table Series, 1990.)
"Simply This" (René Magritte. *The Double Secret*, 1927.)
"In My Dream" (Franz Marc. *The Tower of Blue Horses*, 1913.)
"At the Amphitheater in Mission Dolores Park" (Amei Papitto. *Mission Dolores Park*, 2022.)

"Flawed Photos Must Suffice" (Odilon Redon. *Composition Fleurs*.)

Hybrid Forms:

"What the Country Wrought" - Haibun

Created by Japanese poet, Matsuo Basho, in the 17th century, haibun combines a prose poem with one or more haiku. The haiku usually ends the poem as an insightful postscript that links to the prose that begins the poem.

"Diving" - Zuihitsu

Sei Shōnagon, a medieval courtier, originated this distinctly Japanese form, a piece of writing that creates the illusion of being random and erratic, in The Pillow Book. The piece may contain lists, diary entries, conversations, quotations, non-literary information, opinions.

Further Inspiration:

"Ode to the American Black Cowboy" is written for Inspire Spiritual Community's commemoration of Black History Month 2023.

"I Never Knew I So Loved Annis" is written after Dean Rader.

"Oh, My Hips" is written after Lucille Clifton.

"Behold September" is written after Lucia Perillo.

"Resilience" is published in my first collection, You Can't Have It All: Poems (2019)

Acknowledgments

Thank you to the editors of the following publications in which these poems or their early versions appeared:

Rigorous: "The Asterisk" and "Thank You for Your Service"
Mom Egg Review: "Two Daughters, Twice Blessed"
Snapdragon Journal: "Five & Dime Memories"
Cirque Journal: "In the Community Garden" (formerly "Not Invisible")
Writing Covid: "Flawed Photos Must Suffice" (formerly "Celebration") and "Mayday in May 2020"

§

Thank you to my teacher, poet and coach Erin Redfern for your wisdom and guidance in ordering and editing these poems and for being the catalyst for many of them. I have learned so much from you over these past two-and-a-half years.

Thank you to friend, writer, teacher, and coach Joan Raymond of *A Heart for Writing* for sharing your publishing experience and talents in designing this book and bringing it into the world. Thank you for holding my hand through this process.

Thank you to artist, poet and son-in-love Jonathan Swerdlick for allowing me to use your extraordinary painting, *Pavilions*. I fell in love with it immediately, and when it came time to design my book cover, I knew this would be the art.

Thank you to photographer and friend Jill Hayner-Thompson for your time, photo shoot ideas, and skill at making me feel at ease and look good.

Thank you to dear friend Dennis VanderWerff. You are and have always been my sounding board and "bookend" buddy. I appreciate you helping me stay aligned with my goals.

Thank you to my beta readers Michelle Jones, Kathy Payton, and Jennifer Wilson for, as Anne Lamott says, "inspecting every tooth." I appreciate your diligence and skill.

Thank you to Laurel Benjamin for inviting me to join the Ekphrastic Facebook Group and for your thoughtful and provocative curating of photos that stimulated my imagination and were the launch of many poems in this collection.

Thank you to my treasured Red Ferns, Writers of Kern, and Ekphrastic poetry groups and to workshop classmates and leaders for your encouraging comments and insightful suggestions, and for sharing your talents. Each of you has inspired me to continue writing.

Thank you to Frances and Paul Klippel, First Tuesday Poets of Florence, and all who attended open mics and events where I've read. Your enthusiastic reception buoyed my confidence.

Thank you to the good folks at A Very Important Meeting (AVIM). Being settled by your meditations, spending uninterrupted writing time, and becoming enriched by the community were all instrumental in the completion of this work.

Thank you to my cherished ones, my beloveds: wife Judy, daughters Amina and Asila, and brother Thomas. Your belief in me, support, and love mean the world to me and keep me uplifted.

About the Author

Annis Cassells is a poet, writer, teacher, and life coach. She was born and raised in Detroit, Michigan and taught for many years in Bakersfield, California. Annis now splits her time between Bakersfield and Coos Bay, Oregon, writing and conducting memoir writing workshops for senior adults and poetry workshops for aspiring poets. Her occasional blog features articles about writing, stories, and poetry.

In 2019 Annis published her first poetry collection, *You Can't Have It All: Poems*. She contributed seven poems in the 2020 social justice anthology *ENOUGH "Say Their Names…" Messages from Ground Zero to the World*.

Having missed traveling during the Pandemic years, Annis longingly remembers the times she traversed the USA on her trusty Candy Apple Red motorcycle. She compensates by attending writing workshops and poetry readings in far-away places over Zoom.

Discover more:
  https://heyannis.wordpress.com.
  www.connectionsandconversations.com

  facebook.com/AnnisCassellsWriter
  instagram.com/heyannisc

Also by Annis Cassells

You Can't Have It All: Poems (2019)

ENOUGH "Say Their Names..." Messages from Ground Zero to the WORLD
(Anthology, 2020)

The Cassells Kids (Easter 1955)

Made in the USA
Las Vegas, NV
14 August 2023